ADDING PROFIT BY ADDING PURPOSE

ADDING PROFIT BY ADDING PURPOSE

The CFO's CSR Handbook

DEVIN D. THORPE

Adding Profit by Adding Purpose
The CFO's CSR Handbook

ISBN-13: 978-1530869541
ISBN-10: 1530869544

Also by Devin D. Thorpe

- Your Mark on the World: Stories of service that show us how to give more with a purpose without giving up what's most important.

- 925 Ideas to Help You Save Money, Get Out of Debt and Retire a Millionaire So You Can Leave Your Mark on the World

- Crowdfunding for Social Good: Financing Your Mark on the World

Acknowledgements

WHILE YOU MAY imagine the work of writing a book to be a solitary task—my first book truly was—this book was a tremendous collaboration over three years. Beginning with a survey of corporate social responsibility in 2013 and hundreds of interviews with people since, I am merely the scribe. The insights come from people around the globe; for your benefit, I've tried to infer the most logical conclusions.

Most of the stories and insights in this book—and many others I've collected—can be found in my work as a new media journalist, including my 300+ Forbes pieces you can read at forbes.com/sites/devinthorpe. Over the past three years, I've conducted nearly 700 video interviews that were broadcast live over the internet and are recorded. You can find them all at YouTube.com/devinthorpe. I am grateful to the many hundreds of people who have shared their insights with me.

While my guests include a few household names, like Tony Robbins and Steve Young, most are people who are best described as ordinary people doing remarkable things, like Vivian Harr, the nine-year-old girl who raised $100,000 to fight child slavery. Their generosity toward me has inspired my work.

Nancy Mahon, Senior Vice President, Global Philanthropy and Corporate Citizenship for Estée Lauder, joined me twice for live interviews posted to Forbes. MAC Cosmetics, an Estée Lauder brand, operates what is unequivocally the most effective corporate social responsibility program I've found in my research. This book simply wouldn't be what it is without Nancy's support.

As the book began to take shape, I had some early readers work their way through early, incomplete drafts to help me shape it. These include Pearl Wright, Sunnie Giles and Ashok Choudhury. Their feedback unequivocally helped to make the book better.

My wife, Gail has always been both my first and last reviewer, and a sounding board for many of the ideas in the book. It wouldn't be much of an exaggeration to give her coauthor status on this book. I admire her wit, intellect and discernment; I am in awe of her patience.

Of course, notwithstanding all of the help I've had in creating this book, I am solely responsible for its conclusions and the mistakes.

Contents

Introduction

HAVING HAD A 25-year career in corporate finance, culminating as the CFO for the third largest company listed on the 2009 Inc. 500 list, I've written this little corporate social responsibility (CSR) handbook principally for my CFO colleagues. That said, I hope it will be helpful to others as well.

Remembering how time constrained I felt as a corporate executive, I've sought to make the guide highly efficient. The chapters are short and the information is actionable. My goal for the book is to allow you to read it and to launch your own CSR or purpose program in your company.

Chapter 6 is written to help people who work elsewhere in an organization but who want to make a change in the world and want it to work from their current company and for the benefit of their current employer.

The premise of the book is that a CSR program must be profitable in order to do any good and that one that is profitable can do infinite amounts of good. As much as I'd like to say that adding purpose always adds profit, you must do it right to get both profits and social impact.

Even those who are most confident that their purpose programs create profits have some difficulty proving it. The most compelling arguments seem to be that businesses, once they add effective CSR programs, become more profitable. I challenge you not to take profits on faith, but to thoughtfully and strategically measure the bottom line results of your purpose programs. Others, and I, are convinced that you can make the good you do profitable.

The basis for my views come from talking to CSR executives, social entrepreneurs, impact investors and from my own experience as a CFO, investment banker and corporate treasurer. For the past several years, I've been writing about social entrepreneurship—the marriage of business and social impact—for *Forbes* (forbes.com/sites/devinthorpe). I've also been doing a live show where I interview luminaries like number 1 New York Times bestselling author Tony Robbins, Hall of Fame Quarterback Steve Young, billionaires Jean Case and Shari Arison and CEOs from companies like Overstock.com, HSNi, RBC Wealth Management – US and Hyundai USA.

You don't know me and have no reason to trust me as an expert. Trust the CEOs I've come to know and that time and again assure me that driving social impact can help drive profits.

Before we get started, I want to alert you to one of the critical keys to success at creating profits. You personally have to care about the cause your company chooses in order for your efforts to drive either profit or social impact.

Consumers and employees have built in BS detectors. If you roll out a weak-sauced, half-baked, effort with no heart, your community will see through your effort and it will backfire. You will diminish your profits and tarnish your brand.

Speaking to you personally, I'm convinced that capitalism is good and more importantly that capitalists are good. I trust you.

I'm counting on you to identify a cause that you and your people genuinely care about and have resources to address. You do care. So do your people. Together, you can use your combined resources of time, expertise and money to have a big impact on the world for good.

As a final note before getting into the substance of the book, let me provide a simple outline for what's coming. Chapter 1 is makes the case that adding purpose can add profits to your business. The heart of the discussion explaining how to create an effective, profitable CSR program in your company is in chapters 2 through 5. Chapter 6, as noted above, is written for rank and file employees to learn how to launch an effort that will have impact without drawing the ire of the CFO. Chapter 7 will give you some insights on marketing. Chapter 8 is a challenge to hold yourself accountable both for creating the profit and the impact you target. Chapter 9 is a reminder that for all of the talk of profits in the book, you shouldn't lose sight of the fact that a good CSR program will allow you to actually change the world for good. Chapter 10 is a case study describing the most effective CSR program I've found. Finally, the book ends with a quick conclusion reiterating the harmony between profit and impact and the power of profit to drive impact.

Chapter 1

Purpose *Can* Add Profits

BEFORE WE BEGIN in earnest, let's settle on some definitions that will be important to our mutual understanding. I'm going to use several phrases interchangeably throughout this book: purpose, social purpose, mission, social mission, social responsibility and corporate social responsibility. I like the word "social" as a modifier as it is intended to clarify that the objective is to create a societal benefit.

Some others will use the words "purpose" and "mission" in other contexts with substantially dissimilar meanings. To some, these words simply recognize that a company has a customer focus, or that they exist to solve a particular consumer or business problem, that is, to build a better golf ball retriever or a faster computer. There is nothing wrong with such uses of those words nor anything wrong with companies that identify a problem, create a solution and profit from it. That is the very essence of free enterprise and I am a big fan.

In this book, however, when we talk about purpose and mission, let's understand that we're talking about solving social problems and not just market problems. One of the great insights of the last 30 years now gaining massive traction is that solving social problems has a market, which creates opportunities for entrepreneurs and entrepreneurial organizations.

Now, as we begin our work together to add profits to your enterprise, we must first test the hypothesis that adding mission or purpose to our enterprise can add profits. It is important to note that simply adding a social purpose to your business won't necessarily raise it profits, but doing so in a strategic way can.

In fact, successful corporate social responsibility professionals are beginning to appreciate that their programs must be additive to the bottom line or they will be limited in scope to a rounding error on the financial statement with a budget so small that their existence doesn't matter to the organization, thus dooming the mission as well. In contrast, a program that helps drive profits can flourish limitlessly, growing in scale and impact.

Better People

The first evidence of improving profitability for companies that have successfully integrated purpose into their businesses is in their employees. Such companies report having happier, more productive and generally better employees.

For my Forbes page, in 2013, I conducted a standardized interview or survey with 59 corporate representatives to learn about successful corporate social responsibility programs and the benefits that accrue to the corporations. Three key observations came out of the survey:

1. 86 percent said their employees were happier

2. 59 percent said their employees were more productive

3. 76 percent said they ended up with better employees

Let's explore what they told us.

To anyone who has ever volunteered time, it is not surprising that employers report that their purpose programs increase the happiness of their employees. We experience that when we take time to give. A Gallup Survey in 20141 found that people who volunteer in their communities score significantly higher on the Well-Being Index, with scores of 70 compared to less-giving with scores of 58. That represents more than a 20 percent increase in well-being associated with helping in their communities.

This survey just confirms what we already knew from our own experiences as volunteers. When we give we get. When we serve others we feel better. When we actively engage our employees in a service, they are happier.

It was more surprising to me that companies reported that adding a social mission to the business improved the productivity of their employees. After all, we talking about a program that deliberately asks employees to take their eye off the ball and focus on something external to the business for some, typically limited, part of the time.

Still, 59 percent of the companies who responded to my *Forbes* survey indicated that their employees were more productive as a result of adding purpose.

This is consistent with research from Northwestern University published in 2012 that showed that the more effectively a com-

---

1   Gallup, "Americans Serving Their Communities Gain Well-Being Edge," August 12, 2014, Lindsey Sharpe (http://bit.ly/1GmPdBt).

pany engages in three aspects of corporate giving, the more engaged the employees become, noting, "the more committed an organization is to breadth and depth of their corporate citizenship programming and the more hands on employees can be, the higher their engagement scores."[2]

The final observation of my *Forbes* survey was that companies reported having better employees as a result of both being able to screen employees more effectively and by being able to develop them more effectively.

A 2008 study conducted by David Montgomery at UC Santa Barbara and reported by Stanford showed that MBA students at 11 of the country's top schools, were willing to give up an average of 14 percent of their potential salary to work for an organization whose values were aligned with their own.[3]

Consider the implications of this. If the people we stereotypically think of as being the most cynical people on the planet—top MBA students—are in fact willing to give up a substantial portion of their salaries to work at a company that better reflects their values, what would the average engineer or marketing person be willing to give up? Further consider the power you have in recruiting once you have fully and effectively built purpose into the DNA of your organization. You get to pick the cream of the crop!

Similarly, the employees you have already are going to have development opportunities by virtue of your mission. Their time spent organizing, planning and executing service will give them experience and perspective that they may get in no other way, allowing them to develop skills that you can utilize every day.

---

2   Northwestern University, "How Corporate Citizenship Impacts Employee Engagement," June 2012, Sarah Ketvirtis (http://bit.ly/1eOu64M).

3   Stanford, "For MBA Grads, Corporate Responsibility Trumps Salary," June 1, 2008, Bill Snyder,

Art Papas, the CEO of Bullhorn, gives employees one day each quarter to volunteer. The company's software is used to support recruiters so the company works with nonprofits that focus on ending working-class poverty. Papas said, "These efforts demonstrate to employees that we share their personal values. It changes the employment relationship—it's not just about a pay check, it's about working together to accomplish something."

Similarly, John Taft, the CEO of RBC Wealth Management US, a wealth management firm with over $200 billion in assets under management said, "Employees want to work with a company that they respect."

Taken together, we can see exactly how adding mission to our efforts can help us find and develop happier and more productive employees while giving ourselves the opportunity to recruit better employees as we grow.

More and More Loyal Customers

Customers are people, too, and they will respond to appropriate purpose programs with resounding support.

Teresa Bowman, my stylist—please don't blame her for the way I look, she doesn't have much to work with—recently discovered this. After attending a community council meeting where the Police Chief, Chris Burbank, was fielding questions about the homeless from downtown business owners when he flipped the tables, suggesting that if every business owner just did a little to help the homeless, the problems with them would quickly be eliminated.

Teresa took that to heart and began doing simple makeovers for women at the Road Home Shelter in Salt Lake City. She immediately fell in love and began going weekly to the shelter to do hair.

She was joined by some of her stylists and over time they began to get to know the women they were helping, seeing them make progress as they were lifted simply by having someone care for and respect them.

Over the first six months of her efforts, she hired two of the women to work in her salon and helped a third find a job. Not bad for a program that takes just a few hours one night a week.

KUTV, the local CBS television affiliate, got wind of her work and did a story on the 10:00 news as part of their ongoing "Pay it Forward" segment. Typically, the station profiles the work of non-profit organizations for the segment and a representative of Mountain America Credit Union presents the nonprofit with a check for $500. Departing just a bit from the standard script, they presented Teresa with a check for $500 to help her continue her work with the homeless.

The value of that exposure to the MidCity Salon is difficult to measure, but it has certainly been dramatically positive. Her phone buzzed for days with messages from friends and customers. It is hard to imagine going anywhere else to have my hair cut now that my stylist is so well known for doing good.

This example helps to illustrate what my Forbes survey found. A large minority, 42 percent of the companies responding, said that they had observed higher sales as a result of their mission-related efforts. A solid 70 percent said that they had more loyal customers due to their purpose programs.

This is consistent with data from Nielsen[4], indicating that 55 percent of global consumers were willing to pay a premium for

---

4   Nielsen Global Survey, "Global Consumers Are Willing To Put Their Money Where Their Heart Is When It Comes To Goods And Services From Companies Committed To Social Responsibility," June 17, 2014, (http://bit.ly/1V8t-FUg).

products they considered socially responsible. North Americans were the least likely among global consumers to be willing to pay a premium, but even then, a large minority—40 percent, representing over 100 million people—were willing to pay more.

The Nielsen survey also noted that the respondents had already made sustainable purchases; 52 percent of the total, representing the vast majority of those who said they would be willing to buy such products, already had.

Increasingly, people are trying to use the influence their money gives them to have a positive impact on the world, not only with gifts to nonprofits, but increasingly in their investments and purchases as well.

A Harvard experiment reported in the Economist[5] demonstrates the point. In the experiment, towels were labeled with the following message:

> These towels have been made under fair labour conditions, in a safe and healthy working environment which is free of discrimination, and where management has committed to respecting the rights and dignity of workers.

The researchers monitored the sales and periodically increased the price of the towels, which were sold alongside identical towels without the fair labor label. The result is that the towels with the label outsold the others even after each successive price increase. While the article concludes that it is difficult to get it just right for your customers, there is good reason today to be socially minded.

The bottom line on the top line is that revenue is quite likely to be positively impacted by being more socially responsible. This

---

5   "The good consumer," Jan 17, 2008, (http://econ.st/1DrFa3j).

comes from several factors, including your appeal to new customers, more loyal, repeat buyers and the potential to increase your prices. Given the steady trend toward greater sustainability and a purpose orientation among consumers over the last thirty years, we can reasonably expect the trend to continue.

Eliminating Waste

Following World War II, a Yale trained physicist by the name of William Edwards Deming went to Japan at the behest of General McArthur to help companies seeking to rebuild. His work focused on statistical process control for measuring quality. He is regarded by many to be the father of the Japanese penchant for exceptional quality and efficiency, which have been copied around the world, including here in the U.S. Lean manufacturing, which grew out of Deming's work, has been extended to computer programming and even the process for starting a business with generally positive effect.

Much of that work centers on the elimination of waste, principally as a means to improve profitability. If a finished product can't be sold, that is a tremendous waste of effort, raw materials and profits. It is also a tragic waste of energy and natural resources. Seen through the lens of sustainability, the objective may change, but the goal does not: eliminate waste.

As a gauge of people's interest in reducing waste for environmental reasons, consider that since 1960, municipal solid waste recycling has increased five-fold as a percentage of the total.[6] This suggests a tectonic shift in attitudes about the environment.

---

6   Solid Waste District, 2012, "Garbage Statistics and Studies," (http://bit. ly/1DrBdMl).

One key implication of growing support for environmentalism is that you should organize your waste reduction efforts and reporting so that your employees, customers and shareholders are all aware of your efforts to become more environmentally friendly. This is likely to create a virtuous cycle, as employees and customers work with you to further reduce any adverse environmental impacts and to collectively seek positive environmental impacts.

When I spoke with Nature Conservancy CEO Mark Tercek about the role of business in protecting the environment, he pointed me to his book, *Nature's Fortune, How Business and Society Thrive in Nature,* which includes a powerful example of self-interested environmentalism.

Coca-Cola, according to Tercek, didn't list water as an ingredient in its 2002 10K, the annual report filed with the Securities and Exchange Commission (SEC). As global environmentalism increased, however, and the company faced increased reputational and practical risks related to access to clean water sources around the world for bottling its products, the tone of the annual report changed. In 2010, according to Tercek, the annual report listed water first under the section heading, "Raw Materials." The report noted that water was the primary ingredient in substantially all of the company's products.

Coke didn't stop there. In 2007, the company pledged to become "water neutral," returning to nature and the community the same amount of water it uses in its products. Pepsi, not to be outdone, has pledged to become water positive, returning more water than it uses.

Once Coke and Pepsi began to see water as a finite resource and key ingredient in their products, their approach to managing that resource changed. Certainly, there is an element of genuine concern for the environment, but environmental efforts at the scale undertaken by these beverage behemoths can only be justified economically. While neither Tercek nor I were in the room for those discussions, one can easily conclude there is a financial return on the investment in protecting safe water supplies.

"That's something I'm able to prove!"

Shari Arison is a Forbes-listed billionaire and one of the richest women in the world. She is passionate about doing good, whether that is at a personal level where kindness should prevail or at the corporate level.

During a visit with her earlier this year, I asked her if she believed that incorporating corporate social responsibility programs into business was profitable.

Her response was remarkable. She said, "That's something I'm able to prove!" She went on to explain that she had incorporated a 13-point standard of goodness into her businesses and had watched profits increase.

Given the evidence, there can be no doubt that a properly implemented purpose program can increase the profitability of a venture. In the rest of the book, we'll focus on how you effectively implement a program so that it does increase your profits.

Chapter 2

Choose Authentically

THE FIRST KEY to successfully implementing a CSR program is to choose a cause authentically.

For some organizations, a cause may be fairly obvious. For instance, a veterinarian could choose to support no kill animal shelters and a plastic surgeon who specializes in breast augmentation might choose breast cancer as a cause. Other situations may not lend themselves so obviously to a cause. Other, random factors may put a cause in your bath that you simply can't step over or around.

BDA, a sports marketing firm, had their cause thrust upon them in the most tragic way imaginable.

In 2011, the BDA team took a company trip to Kona, Hawaii. While there, Susan, a member of the team, was brutally murdered by her "boyfriend." Though colleagues could hear her screaming before she died, they couldn't get into the room in time to save her. The boyfriend was arrested and just before trial in June 2012, he pled guilty to second-degree murder. In December of that year, he was sentenced to life in prison.

The firm's BDA Cares Foundation has a special page on its website dedicated to Susan and her story. It says, in part, "We lost Susan. Nothing can bring her back. But we can keep her spirit alive by helping others avoid and escape this terrible crime. At BDA, we have made a commitment to make a difference and we will stand alongside victims and their families until this epidemic is stopped. We will be their rock."

Domestic violence has become the primary cause at BDA, reflecting the employees' collective concern for their lost friend and fueling their passion for actually making a difference in the lives of people who are at risk of becoming victims.

Employee Input

Your employees will likely be asked to volunteer time both while they are on the clock and off the clock and to donate money to your cause. They can be great partners. While it is most common for senior management teams, most often the CEO, to make the final decision about a CSR program, you'll really want to have buy in from your employees so that you can maximize your impact.

In order to get buy in, you'll want to start by getting their input first, even if you think you know what the cause should be. Of course, if the CEO knows what the cause is going to be, that is, the decision has been made, don't fake the process of seeking input. Your employees will see right through it.

You'll probably want to start with a survey to gauge employees' interest in possible causes. You'll definitely want to structure your survey in a way that does not imply that causes that simply aren't on the table for consideration are on the table. For instance, if you operate an animal testing lab, you wouldn't want to give your employees the sense that ending animal testing is on the table.

You could start by asking employees to choose among eight broad categories of nonprofits such as the following:

- **Animals** (endangered species, animal cruelty, shelters, etc.)

- **Arts and Culture** (art, museums, cinema, theater, dance, symphony, etc.)

- **Education** (universities, public schools, private schools, special needs schools, schools for the impoverished, etc.)

- **Environment** (climate change, pollution, urban planning, etc.)

- **Health** (cancer, diabetes, cystic fibrosis, malaria, polio, HIV/AIDS, etc.)

- **Human Rights** (torture, political prisoners, women's rights, democracy, etc.)

- **Orphans** (foster care, big brothers/big sisters, special needs children, Chinese orphans, poverty-driven orphanages)

- **Poverty** (global hunger, local food banks, homelessness, income distribution, etc.)

- **Religion** (many consider their religion a cause; many religions provide humanitarian relief)

Most employers will quickly decide to omit religion from the list to avoid the potential divisions that might cause. Some management teams, for a variety of reasons, might choose to narrow the list further.

It would be wise to ask employees to respond with a scaled response and not just a yes or no. You not only want to know if they would be willing to support a cause, but whether they are enthusiastic about one. Similarly, you need to know if your employees have strong negative feelings—or at least if some do—about particular causes.

You'll also want to ask open-ended questions to learn what motivates their support for particular causes. The employees may see a strategic connection to a cause that you've overlooked.

Once you've surveyed the employees, you may want to assemble some formal or informal focus groups to better understand the team's feelings about adopting a cause. In an informal focus group, you might sit down with a group of employees yourself to talk about their interests, passions and motivations related to a cause. If you have the budget, however, you'll get more honest responses by hiring someone else to conduct the sessions so they are not influenced by your presence or your own biases.

The process of gathering input from your employees will also give you an opportunity to find champions, leaders you can harness to help you roll out the program among the rank and file. Without that support, a new initiative like this can die before it even gets rolling. Be sure to note what fires the passion of the individual leaders. Some may be excited to have a purpose initiative of any sort to get behind, while others may be excited about one thing that is near and dear to their hearts but complacent about other causes. Make notes about these things so you can call upon the truly passionate for the cause you ultimately choose.

As you seek to engage your employees, work to get some input from as many as possible, to get thoughtful feedback from a few and to identify the leader who can help you roll this out.

Customer Input

You don't just need your employees' backing, you also want the enthusiastic support of your customers. You want to choose something that they care about as well. To find out what they care about, you'll need to ask them, too.

Just like you did with your employees, you can use polls and focus groups to gather information from your customers. This makes sense if you have hundreds, thousands or millions of customers. On the other hand, if you have relatively few clients, you may want to talk to them one-on-one instead.

Your approach for learning about customer interests will likely vary significantly based on whether your customers are consumers or businesses. Even a small business with consumers as customers will likely have hundreds of customers. Large businesses may have millions. Large businesses probably won't choose even to survey all of the customers, but will survey a sampling instead to get a sense of what they care about.

Surveys can be supplemented by focus groups, just as you might have done with your employees. Small businesses may choose to lead informal discussions with a group of customers. Large businesses may hire professionals to gather groups and tease out their real passions in a scientific way.

A small business, however, that serves other businesses may have only a few customers. A large business with many businesses as customers can approach them much like a consumer business would with surveys and focus groups.

If you run a small business with relative few business customers, you may simply want to ask your customers if they would be interested in engaging with you on a mission-related effort to improve the world or the community. Some may pass without learning any more, but most are likely at least to ask what you have in mind.

At this stage, you may not be ready to give specifics—and that's fine—use this opportunity to ask your customer what they are already doing at their shop. Whatever they tell you can be valuable information. If they are scattered, doing a variety of things, they'd likely be willing to engage or at least to appreciate what you ultimately choose to do regardless of what it is.

If a customer has a well-developed program that fits with the interests of your employees, you may want to look at projects that relate or even to join your customer in their project. If it is a key customer, it could be highly strategic to build your relationship by joining their cause.

If your customer says they are not doing anything, don't assume that they don't necessary want to do something. The effort required to go from nothing to something is daunting. You may be able to engage them easily down the road by making their participation in your program painless.

Harmonizing Differing Perspectives

At this point, you are likely to have two and perhaps three different perspectives. You may have your own perspective, we'll think of that as the management perspective. You should also have an employee view of the issue and a customer view. Your goal now is to harmonize those perspectives in a way that will respect the inputs you've received and allow you to go forward successfully.

There is a real advantage in choosing the most popular initiative, even if it isn't management's first choice. By picking a popular option, you reduce the amount of work you'll need to do to get people on board with the new purpose program. You can build the same kind of passion the BDA employees had for domestic violence after Susan's murder, by fanning the flames that are already burning in your customers and employees. Finding passion is easier than creating passion!

You can tap into the employee and customer leaders who are already fired up to help you roll the program out. They can serve as early volunteers for the cause, spokespeople for the effort and help you rally more troops.

While there is great data to suggest that people who give back are far happier, remember that some of your employees may already be giving back in far more committed ways, perhaps to other causes. I've occasionally seen people get angry and frustrated with colleagues or even spouses because they won't join the right cause. When someone declines to engage in a corporate purpose program, you'd be wise to assume that it's because they are fully committed to another cause. In the long run, such people will likely be warmed into your effort and may actually do more than others do given their practiced abilities at service.

If you can't get behind the most popular option, or if there is no clear winner, you may be forced to choose something for which there wasn't a great deal of support. To get your employees and customers behind it, you'll want to be as transparent as possible. You may need to show survey results showing that there wasn't a clear winner or that the clear winner isn't feasible. Be careful to avoid a cause with a relatively high negative feedback from employees or customers.

For instance, if the clear winner for a company was providing famine relief in Africa and you run a small business, you could make the executive decision that compelling as that cause is, the company's ability to make a difference is too limited. You might, instead, look to do something to alleviate hunger right in your own community. A small company can make a big difference in reducing hunger in the local community.

Whatever you choose, you've got to be ready to make a connection between the cause you choose and your customers and employees. They need to feel as if you've considered their input and chosen wisely rather than arbitrarily. A customer who feels like her input was valued, even if not heeded, will be much more likely to support your cause—and your business—going forward.

By involving your employees and customers in the process of choosing a cause for your purpose program you increase the probability of being able to create a successful program that will both have a meaningful measurable impact on the problem you hope to solve and to create a positive impact on the bottom line. To achieve that, you want to find or create the sort of genuine connection between the cause and the company that the employees of BDA felt after Susan's murder.

Chapter 3

Scale Appropriately

HAVING CHOSEN A cause, you need to begin thinking about implementing action that is appropriate to your scale. You, guided by your employees to choose a massive social issue, may be thinking how can our little company make a dent in a global problem?

Every company, large or small, needs to begin thinking about corporate responsibility initiatives at the proper scale for their company. The proper scale will be a function of many factors, including revenue, profit margins and number of employees. Until you've proven that your implementation of a purpose program is driving profits higher, most stake holders will want to be sure you've limited the company's financial exposure. That is as it should be. Once you have proven that the program increases profits you will likely get permission to grow the program and its impact.

For many organizations, there is a popular benchmark for setting scale. By seeking to create a program that represents 1 percent of the company's time, 1 percent of its money and 1 percent of its expertise, companies are finding that they can have a huge impact. Some companies talk about the three Ts, Time, Treasure and Talent.

It may seem ironic at first, but the largest companies have the most difficult time reaching this level of contribution — though some certainly do. The smallest businesses have the easiest time and may be able to exceed these goals, perhaps materially.

Don't think of the 1 percent goal as an upper or lower bound on your program; consider it a starting point and gauge in your own organization how that would feel.

Think about your corporate social responsibility program as a bathing suit. You want it to be comfortable to allow you to swim and you want to look as good as possible given that you'll be wearing it in public. If the suit is too big, loose and baggy it could fall off when you jump in the water — your CSR program may not survive its own launch. On the other hand, if it is too small, it may cover too little and leave you in an embarrassing situation — picture a Fortune 500 executive proudly presenting to a nonprofit a giant-size cardboard check for $100. The gesture would reveal and highlight the company's penurious nature rather than give it a generous image. Scale in a purpose program is as important as choosing the right size bathing suit.

Find a Problem and Fix It

Once you have identified a cause, you need to begin thinking about the action you'll take. In order to fire passions, you want to stay away from a generic fundraising for charity approach. Don't get me wrong, money can and should be a key part of your effort, but simply throwing money at a large, national nonprofit may fail to fuel the passion of your employees and customers.

Instead, you want to look for a specific project that your organization can tackle. Look for a project that will fit in your sandbox and allow you to make it into a castle.

For instance, if your cause is to improve education for underprivileged children in your community, rather than donate funds generically to the local education foundation, you could instead meet with the local school principal and identify a specific project that needs to be completed, whether that is buying a new copier, upgrading the playground or providing tutors for specific, at-risk children. Once you've identified the project, then you'll want to develop a plan—with the help of your team—to actually solve the problem. You'll want to do something that will allow you to say at some point in the future, "mission accomplished." Then you can repeat the process.

By suggesting this, I don't mean for a moment to limit the size of the project. A company selling beverages to consumers in virtually every country on the planet is selling to millions upon millions of people who will get malaria. About half a million of them will die every year. It isn't too much to tackle for a global corporation to dedicate some of their money, time and expertise to battling malaria. The disease won't be eradicated in a week, a year or even a decade, but it can be eradicated and it could easily become the rallying point for employees and customers of a global corporation as progress is marked in partnership with the Bill and Melinda Gates Foundation and others already engaged in the fight.

So let's talk about finding projects at the right scale.

Small Companies

In small businesses and micro-enterprises, the ability to give more than 1 percent comes simply from the fact that 1 percent of revenue may be a pretty small number and you may feel you have the ability to do more than that. A small business with $500,000 of revenue would measure 1 percent as $5,000. Many individuals give more than $5,000 to charity in a year and a small business owner may feel comfortable going far beyond that level.

The same principles may also apply to time. If a company has just four or five employees, you may all feel like you can allow your employees to each take one day per quarter to volunteer in the community, considerably more than 1 percent of their time.

Once you have identified your cause and gauged your scale, you are in a good position to look for a project. Following the mantra, "find a problem and fix it," you can contact small nonprofits in your community to discuss projects your company can tackle.

There are many small nonprofits. A quick google search should allow you to find a list of the nonprofits in your community. Most states have an association of nonprofits with a website that will list at least all of the member nonprofits if not all nonprofits in your state. Your local community foundation may also publish a list. If you are looking for a small project, small nonprofits are likely to be most eager for your help. Many have budgets under $100,000 per year and are run mostly by volunteers. They will be eager for any help you can offer.

Note, too, that if your passions are international, you may still be able to find a locally-based, small nonprofit eager to have help with a discrete project in a far flung part of the developing world. Visiting the country and the project may not be necessary, but could be a fun part of the project if you like traveling in the developing world.

Be sure to involve enough employees in the process that that you have a good sense of their appetite for any work that may be involved. When you give employees a day off to volunteer on the project, you want them to be excited about the opportunity.

Medium Companies

Based on my experience as the CFO and my observations as a journalist, medium sized companies, those with between $100 million and $1 billion in revenue are those most likely to find the 1 percent model a closer fit. Doing more than that can put strain on the organization. Doing less may feel inadequate to your employees and your customers. If you are starting from scratch, however, it may not be reasonable to go from zero to spending $1 million or more annually on your cause.

There are ways, however, to have $1 million of impact without spending $1 million of cash. Your employees and customers are likely willing to chip in. If you have 500 employees in your company, collecting just $10 per month per employee adds $60,000 to the pot.

If you can donate two days of their time during the year to volunteer, you are spending another $100,000 (500 x 2 x $100 typical daily wage). Remember, we discussed earlier how engaging your employees in a cause they care about makes them happier and more productive. Your donation of their time, done effectively, will come right back to you. You should see more work accomplished even though your employees are also tackling volunteer work. We'll discuss involving your employees further in chapter 4.

You may also be able to donate your product or service. Margins vary, but it isn't unusual for the retail value of a product or service to be three times the cost of producing the service. Perhaps you can donate $500,000 of your product or service over the course of a year in a way that will actually cost you less than

$170,000. Some software venders may be able to give software away nearly for free while still adding tremendous value to their cause.

Finally, your customers are likely to be willing to pitch in. We'll devote chapter 5 of this book to discussing ways to engage your customers. The punch line is this. To get the full benefit of rebranding your company as socially aware, you'll need to ask your customers to help you, to make them partners in your effort.

So far, we've identified the following possible elements of a $1 million initial campaign:

Employee cash contributions:	$ 60,000
Donated employee time:	$ 100,000
Donated product/service:	$ 500,000
Subtotal:	$ 660,000

The subtotal of $660,000 gets you two-thirds of the way to your goal. Can you reasonably hope to get the balance from customers? Certainly. While there are no guarantees and every situation is different, you can hope to engage your customers in a way to get them to help you fund that shortfall, bringing your total first year impact to your target of $1 million with no cash outlay. In this scenario, the only incremental cost is the cost of the donated product. If you have software margins or surplus goods, the impact can be nearly free.

As you prove the impact of the effort on your community and on your business, we'd expect that you can increase your funding to grow your program in such a way that the company can afford to chip in cash to drive significantly more impact. In the abstract, it seems counter intuitive to think about growing spending, but when you think about lives impacted by a genuine and effective program you may find yourself channeling your inner Oscar Schindler, looking for creative ways to increase your impact.

As you think about projects and organizations to support, you may have the resources and ability to tackle a few projects. By focusing on relatively few projects that are closely related you can maximize the messaging and impact. For instance, if you are working on improving educational attainment of girls, you might have a project at a school in Africa and another right in your own community. By putting both projects under one easily identified umbrella you can aggregate your impact statistics when you talk about what's been accomplished.

Large Companies

Large companies, those with over $1 billion in revenue, will have the hardest time meeting or exceeding the goal to give 1 percent. Don't be down on yourself or your organization. Focus instead on having enough genuine impact to make your employees and customers proud of their association with you.

In a large company, it will make sense to have one or more people devoted full-time to managing your corporate philanthropy. It is imperative to have them work closely with marketing and human resources to ensure that customers and employees are properly involved.

Involvement is really the only way to ensure that your employees and customers actually realize that your company cares about your cause. Just telling them over and over will ring hollow and may be ignored. Get them to contribute a bit of time or money and suddenly you are partners in a cause.

As you develop CSR programs in a large corporation, you'll ultimately end up spending money on many different projects. Your goal should be to build around a theme. RBC Wealth Management US, a $200 billion firm, committed $50 million over seven years to clean water. Over that time they funded dozens of projects and deployed their employees as volunteers across the country on many of them. The projects are as diverse as funding research projects leading to improved technologies for clean water and programs to get underprivileged youth involved in water sports like canoeing to help them connect with their natural habitat.

By sticking to a theme, RBC creates clear branding. Customers and employees know the company is working to make the world a better place by increasing access to clean water and protecting water resources in the environment.

You could do the same thing around a variety of different themes all connected to a cause that you have chosen authentically using the discussion from the last chapter.

Large companies will also need to be diligent about measuring impact. For the sake of both inside and outside audiences, being able to describe the impact of projects and not just the activities is increasingly important. People want to know what happens as a result. If you are cleaning river banks, you want to know what the downstream impact is that you are hoping to achieve and then you need to measure against that goal.

When you are writing five, six and seven figure checks to organizations doing this kind of work, it is reasonable to ask them to report back. You then need to aggregate the impacts data you're receiving.

This challenge is not intended to create a focus on projects with immediate impacts. It is laudable and defensible to undertake projects with time spans of years or even decades. Corporations can last indefinitely and as a result they can tackle long-term projects and measure progress over long spans of time.

Finally, large corporations especially need to measure the profitability or the impact of a purpose program on the bottom line of the enterprise. While it may be difficult to measure the impact of clean water on revenue and profitability, it is important to make an attempt. It is beyond the scope of this book to describe the best practices in this arena, but the best companies with the best programs are making reasonable estimates.

Polling customers and employees should give you insights into their loyalty and how that impacts your business. Public relations metrics can give you a measure of the value of the equivalent marketing dollar that might have been spent. Remember that what others say about you can be much more valuable than what you say about yourself.

Keep Some Powder Dry

For businesses at any scale, you may also want to keep a portion of your purpose budget set aside for strategic, high impact opportunities. Contributing a relatively small amount to a project outside of your cause may make sense in a variety of circumstances.

If the request comes from a key customer or would have a big impact on a community where many of your employees live, it may make great economic sense to step up and play a role suited to the size of the enterprise and the problem. Again, we're talking about relatively small projects compared to your broader purpose program.

Regardless of the size of your enterprise, you'll want to define the process for reviewing requests for funding. In a sole proprietorship, the process may be nothing more than the instructions on your website for making requests, along with some guidance as to what you are likely to fund and at what scale.

For large enterprises, you'll want to define a process for applying for funds, the process by which review and approval is made and the internal and external accountability for proper use of funds and measurement of impact. Mid-size enterprises will want to find the right place on the continuum for the size of the company.

Microsoft v. Bill and Melinda Gates Foundation

Before we continue, I want to draw attention to a potential point of confusion and eliminate it. Some people think of the Bill and Melinda Gates Foundation as the purpose program or corporate social responsibility effort of Microsoft. The connection between the two entities is obvious in that Bill Gates made his fortune becoming the wealthiest person in the world by owning a large stake in and running Microsoft.

That said, Microsoft does not fund the Gates Foundation, Bill and Melinda Gates do. Microsoft reports giving away about $1.1 billion in 2014 on revenue of $86.8 billion or about 1.25 percent of revenue. The bulk of the effort was in the form of free software, but $119 million was cash donations.

The Bill and Melinda Gates Foundation is giving away significantly more each year, but that giving shouldn't properly be considered part of the Microsoft giving.

Other wealthy entrepreneurs have similarly joined the Giving Pledge, promising at least half of their fortunes to charity in recent years as well.[7] Their personal giving shouldn't be an excuse for

---

7   http://givingpledge.org/

the corporations they founded not to give. The personal giving of wealthy entrepreneurs like Bill Gates, Mark Zuckerberg and others should inspire their respective companies to give and not excuse them from giving.

Chapter 4

Involve Your Employees

HAVING GATHERED INPUT from your employees, it is easy to assume away the steps required to engage your employees in your purpose program. Please don't ignore the process for engaging them. Be strategic. In order to build the long-term benefits to the company, you need to have a positive experience among your employees.

Many of the specifics for how you will engage your employees will vary by size of your organization, but there are some guiding principles that will help you regardless of size.

Principle 1: Organize

You need to give your corporate social responsibility program some structure. In a large organization a department could be created just to plan and organize the work associated with your purpose program. In a mid-sized organization, you'll likely have a person devoted primarily or exclusively to running it. In a small company, the program will have to be given to someone with other duties.

Regardless of the size of the organization, you need to find people to lead the project who have a real passion for it. There will be plenty of pressure for the program to be lean and to drive profits, so make sure the leaders are passionate about the impact of the program. You need your other employees to feel a genuine sense of commitment to the cause.

If employees sense that your efforts are hollow, hypocritical or two-faced, you've lost before you begin. Make sure your internal leaders actually want to help you create positive change and impact. The work you've made to choose a cause authentically, should help you to identify the passionate players in your organization.

Once you have a command center formed, you need to begin engaging other employees. You'll want to have between one in 10 and one in 100 employees actively engaged in planning and preparing for work related to the cause, even if it is only fundraising from the employees. Optimally, there will be work to be done, whether it is pro bono professional work, or painting houses on weekends, that all of your employees can engage in.

In a large organization, say one with 10,000 employees, if you have one of every 50 employees engaged in planning and organization that would be 200 employees. That sounds like a lot. At some level, it is, but it may not be enough. In a company of that size, you'll probably be undertaking a variety of projects. If you have 20 projects, that is a committee of merely 10 per project. Remember, you want to spread the work around so that employees feel engage but not overwhelmed. By and large, you'll want to gather volunteers, people who are already excited about the cause.

You want those who are actively engaged in the planning to infect others when it is time for execution. When it is time for employees to head down to the park to pick up trash, clean up a river bank or paint a home for someone in need, you want as many as possible to participate. You want to create a sense that it is a privilege to join in the fun. If some employees have to stay back in the shop to keep the lights on, let them feel that in some way they are doing their part for the cause, too, by making it possible for the others to do some service.

Keep in mind, that an appropriate level of activity in a large organization may be just a one day project, so having a high level of participation could be critical to getting the engagement benefit you're hoping for.

Note, too, that some employees may not catch the vision of your purpose program until they are actually in the thick of it. At some point as they walk along the river banks removing trash by the tons, your group of employees will individually and collectively begin to see the reality of their impact. You've been a real success when your employees return to work talking about next year.

Principle 2: Delegate Because Autonomy Fuels Passion

One of the great opportunities involved in your purpose initiative is the chance to allow employees to develop skills they may not use in their current positions but that would be valuable to the organization. Your purpose program can be led largely by rank and file employees who may not have much if any management experience or training. By delegating responsibility to people who aren't accustomed to having much, you train and enable them to handle more.

Furthermore, when you give employees responsibility and authority to plan and execute your employee activities for your purpose program, you vest them in your program and make them partners. The more they engage in this project with you, the more they become your partners. The benefits that accrue to the company, come largely from increasing the employees' loyalty and enthusiasm for working for the company.

Using the river bank clean up as an example, you may tell your employees to organize in groups and to plan and organize clean ups in manageable groups of up to 50 people. There will be lots of logistics to prepare so it will give them a great challenge. In general, the greater autonomy they feel in choosing a venue, building a team and executing the plan the more positive will be their experience, the more work will be accomplished leading to the most impact.

Here is where gray-haired CFO's like me would see synergy and win-win, except with corporate social responsibility done well, there are at least three winners, including the employees, the company and the community you serve.

Principle 3: Fund the Organizing Effort

Of course, you will almost certainly have to provide some if not all of the programmatic funding for your social purpose, but it may be tempting to ignore or leave unfunded the process of planning and organizing the project.

Nothing will discourage your team faster or bring the project to a quicker halt than refusing to fund the routine costs of setting up the program. Such costs will typically be small, but could include the cost of meals or perhaps just donuts for team meetings, transportation costs, printing costs for signs, banners and mailers, other promotional costs, and other miscellaneous items. Don't let these nuisance costs that mean so little to the bottom line of the organization get in the way of the project by putting them on the employees unnecessarily.

When the employees feel your complete support, they will engage enthusiastically, make progress productively and will execute your vision beyond your expectations.

Give Your Employees Time

Ultimately, you want to include as many people in the project as possible. Whether this happens with all employees on a single day or on a rotating or ad hoc basis doesn't matter much. You do want to give them paid time to engage in the project.

Using 1 percent as a guideline, you might reasonably give your employees two or three full days to work on the project each year. Given that some will spend time organizing and planning and their cumulative time may far exceed that standard, even giving most employees just one or two days would be seen as a reasonable commitment from the company to supporting the project.

While employees are on the clock, they can be strongly encouraged or even required to participate. You'll probably want to give people some sort of escape provision that really works so that employees feel like they have opted in, even if they are pressured to participate. The thinking is that you may need to cajole employees into participating with the hope and expectation that once they have participated they'll feel more positively toward the project and the company. Of course, this could be lost if the employees instead feel forced to participate.

One way to encourage participation is to recognize those who are engaged actively in the project. You want to create a culture that values and respects the people who are doing the most to advance the project.

All who participate in the project should be given some form of recognition, whether that is a hat or t-shirt or a designation on their name tags or cubicles, you want to create a sense of comradery among those who join in the effort.

Ask For Their Time

It is also reasonable to ask your employees who wish to participate to do so on their own time in addition to helping on your time and your dime. Here, it is even more important that this be optional. Those who are most excited about the program can be encouraged and recognized for donating time to the project on their own time.

The closer your connection to an independent nonprofit organization involved in the project, the easier it will be for employees to participate in the project and continue its work without the time and expense of the company's involvement in organizing and planning such efforts.

Many of your employees already devote themselves in meaningful ways to a variety of community-building activities from teaching Sunday school to coaching soccer and from caring for aging parents to caring for their own special-needs children. It is important to be sensitive to their efforts. If you shut down their community activities in order to make time for the company project, the goal of building unity in the ranks could be undone. Optimally, you will not only tolerate but embrace the volunteer work that your employees undertake in whatever form it may take.

Ask for Their Money

Perhaps nothing is more sensitive and fraught with risk than asking your employees to participate in the financial burden of the project.

Your employees can be meaningful financial partners in your effort. This may not come all at once or in big amounts initially, but over time you should be able to collect an amount that could reach 0.5% of your annual payroll. For some companies, that could represent a large portion of the financial goal.

Keep in mind, however, that if employees feel like they are shouldering the bulk of the financial cost of the project, they may not respond as enthusiastically as you'd like. In the best case scenario, the company would offer an explicit match for employee and customer contributions, such that the employees would see that their portion was meaningful, but the smallest of the three sources.

If the project is meaningful to the employees, that is you have chosen authentically as we discussed earlier, and it is being planned and organized effectively, engaging many of the employees in the execution, you are likely to be able to catalyze employee giving at near the target level.

Employees can be reasonably asked to consider donating up to 1 percent of their annual salary. Very few can or will give more than that, so be cautious about communicating any suggestion that they could or should do more than that.

For many, donating one day's compensation would be a stretch. This would be just under 0.5 percent of their annual compensation but may feel more reasonable. For some, giving even one hour's wages will be difficult. You'll want to celebrate the willingness of employees to give anything. Encourage your employees to participate at whatever level they feel most comfortable doing.

Generally, those who read this book will be CFO's or other senior executives. Remember, your household budget is likely to be far different from the budgets of your rank and file employees. While most of your employees are likely to have ample money for food, they may be anxiety ridden over how to pay the school fees every fall or how to outfit three kids for soccer every spring. If they can't figure out how to provide their kids with all of the opportunities they'd like, pressure from you to give "until it hurts" may fall on resentful ears.

Remember, too, that most Americans, in fact, most people in the developed world, are already donating to charitable causes. Too much pressure on your employees to give to an assigned cause could backfire. You don't want to try to convince your employees to give to the company cause instead of the causes they've traditionally supported. Instead, you want to encourage your employees to give a little to the company cause in addition to all of the other good they are already doing.

When you acknowledge your employees are already doing great work and then ask them to do just a little bit more, you make them feel like heroes. By treating your employees like the heroes of the story, you encourage them to do all that they realistically can.

Over time, as your CSR program matures and you accomplish more, your employees will likely want to participate more and more. As they see the success and the impact, they'll want to accelerate and expand it and to claim more credit for it. Be patient. Be positive.

Chapter 5

Engage the Customer

TOM'S SHOES IS one of the great examples of a purpose program that created profits by engaging the customer. Tom's was launched with the one-for-one model where Tom's gives a pair of shoes to a child in need whenever a customer buys a pair of shoes. This captured the attention of media and customers alike and Tom's was an instant sensation. Read the inspiring history by founder Blake Mycoskie, *Start Something that Matters*.

Today, Tom's goes well beyond its one for one program, donating cash to a variety of causes and supporting social entrepreneurs around the world, reflecting a positive and appropriate response to some early criticism of the adverse effects of some forms of giving.

Tom's customers buy the shoes, eyewear, apparel and other merchandise precisely because they know that good comes with the purchase.

There are three primary reasons that you'll want to find creative ways to engage your customers in your own purpose program.

- First, you'll want to share the cost of the program and your customers are likely to be willing to share in the cost.

- Second, by engaging your customers you assure yourself that they know about your collective efforts, building up the value of your brand and growing revenue by extension.

- Third, with the help of your customers you can do more good. By involving them, you not only get their financial support but you may be able to activate some of their volunteer time on behalf of your purpose program and you can certainly increase awareness of the cause, which typically translates into further benefits.

There are an almost unlimited number of ways for you to engage your customers. Don't limit your thinking to the concepts outlined in this book. Instead, brainstorm with your team using the ideas in this book as a starting point.

One creative example I found in my research was the London-based software firm Workshare, which had partnered with Charity: water. Whenever customers—or prospective customers—agree to sit down for an in depth product review (these are not part of the sales cycle but part of the product development process) to provide the company with feedback, Workshare donates $200 to Charity: water. Fifty interviews yield a $10,000 donation that will complete a water project in the developing world that benefits 250 and saves them up to 6,000 hours previously spent collecting water.

The Workshare model is different from most I've found and so I point it out to encourage you to be creative rather than constrained in your thinking. Most of the programs I've studied fall into one of three categories or models for corporate social responsibility.

1. **Percentage of revenue**: In this model, a dedicated (may or may not be published) percentage of revenue is devoted to a social cause.

2. **Token donations**: Here, you ask your customers to make small donations (perhaps as little as pocket change) to a cause in hope that you can aggregate meaningful amounts from lots of customers.

3. **Product proceeds**: Here, you devote part or all of the proceeds from the sale of a product, think bubble gum ice cream at the ice cream counter, to your charitable cause.

Let's look at each of these models in depth to understand how they might be implemented in your shop.

Percentage of Revenue

The Tom's Shoes one-for-one model of giving is a variation on the percentage of revenue. While they never advertise the percentage of revenue they give, their promise to give in accordance with donations is explicit. Even though they don't disclose the percentage of revenue devoted to supporting their causes, you can be assured that they do know what percentage of revenue they devote to their charitable giving programs each year.

The organization One Percent for the Planet requires its corporate members to donate 1 percent of their revenue to causes that support sustainability. Over 1,100 companies have made the pledge and joined the organization. Most of the members are relatively small companies. A few household names, including Patagonia, are on the list.

This model has some particular strengths and weaknesses.

Strengths include the simplicity of the program. Little more than a simple announcement is need to kick off the program. Checks can quickly start flowing once you launch the program and revenues come in. The customers are relatively passive, making the program easy to administer. And, most importantly, some customers will choose to do business with you because of your commitment.

The disadvantages of this model include the fact that customers may not be that impressed, if the percentage given isn't perceived as being sufficient. If you aren't helping enough, you may simply not get the customers' attention. To combat this risk, many companies using this model will publish not the percentage of revenue they donate but the activities they will fund or the impact they will have. In other words, rather than say they will give 1 percent of revenue to support clean water projects in the developing world, they might say that a portion of revenue will go to support clean water projects and that one person will get clean water for every $100 you spend with us.

Token Donations

Lots of companies from the corner drugstore to McDonalds give customers the opportunity to donate loose coins or spare change to a cause, typically by dropping your change into a collection jar. McDonald's has built and supported Ronald McDonald Houses around the country where the families of sick children can stay when visiting cities with quality children's hospitals. For consumer businesses with lots of customers making relatively small and frequent purchases, this model works well.

Another variation on this model is when a company specifically gives you the option to round your total charge up to the nearest dollar with the difference being donated to charity. This frequently happens online and in other situations when customers pay with credit cards.

A similar approach is to charge customers a small amount, say $1 or $5 and to pass the money along to a nonprofit. Often, this approach is paired with an instant recognition. The customer is invited to write a name on a paper cutout related to the cause and the name is posted in the shop window for a few days. The collective effect of dozens or hundreds of donors with their names in the window does convey a sense that lots of people are participating and making a big difference with their small donations.

Let's consider the pros and cons of this model for a moment.

The benefits of this model include that there is only a small commitment required from the customer, allowing many customers to participate. The fact that the customer drops the change in the bucket or buys the window sticker for $1 means that the customer knows that she is participating in your purpose program. Another benefit is the clear potential for creating meaningful impact by aggregating tiny amounts from lots of people.

The drawbacks of the program include that this model doesn't work as well for business to business companies or for companies that make infrequent, large sales to consumers—rounding up the purchase price of a car to the nearest dollar wouldn't generate much money over the course of the year because a dealership sells many fewer cars than McDonald's sells hamburgers. There is another subtle problem here. If the company is purely acting as an aggregator of customer donations for the benefit of a nonprofit, the donors may not value the role of intermediary sufficiently to create the branding benefit you're seeking. The solution may be to match customer donations in some way so that the customers see themselves as partnering with you to do good, giving you the full benefit of the program by giving the customer the good feeling that comes from making a donation and the branding benefit that comes from supporting the cause the customer supports.

Product Proceeds

There is a tremendous amount of flexibility in this model of cause marketing. Not only can you choose the product, you can choose how much of the sales proceeds to devote to the cause. Some organizations will donate all of the revenue from the sale of a particular product. Others will donate a specific dollar amount, usually a portion of the product price. Others still will promise to donate all of the profit from the sale of the products.

New Belgium Brewing created a special glass that they sell to customers for about $5. From the purchase, $1 is donated to one of four causes chosen by the customer. The annual donations made by the company exceed $1 million. By using an add-on product like a glass rather than using one of the company's beverage products, the company protects its margins on its core business. Even if the company isn't making a profit on the glasses, they are actively engaging their customers in their purpose program. Note that they allow the customer to choose the cause. This ensures that each customer who buys a glass understands that she is contributing to a cause by making the purchase. In this way, New Belgium Brewing gets the full branding benefit they hoped to create.

As with the other models, this program has its pros and cons.

This approach provides great flexibility, allowing a company to design the program in a way to maximize customer funding of the social program and to tune it to the company's appetite for scale. Think of it simply, if you have 30 flavors of ice cream in your shop, you likely know how well each flavor sells. You can choose to donate the proceeds from either your best seller or your slowest selling products. You can also choose to donate the revenue, a portion of the revenue or just the profit (or even a percentage of the profit) giving you incredible flexibility for designing your impact.

In addition to the flexibility of the program, you can easily assure yourself that customers actually appreciate that you are donating a portion of the proceeds to a cause by requiring them to choose the cause. This approach guarantees that those who can be influenced by your purpose program are. Furthermore, the commitment you're requiring of the customer is small and comfortable. You're not asking for donations—you make the donation—you're just selling great products.

On the downside, the primary risks come from disappointing the customer. You might be better off to give 100 percent of the profit from an unpopular flavor rather than donate 20 percent of the profit from your most popular. You want your customers to feel that you are making a sacrifice, too. If you choose your most popular products and don't require some level of engagement, like choosing the cause, you run the risk that you'll make a large donation that few customers knew about because they didn't change their purchasing behavior and weren't effectively made aware of the donation. If you choose this approach, be thoughtful about a strategy that will yield the maximum benefit for your cause and for your company.

The program design for your corporate social responsibility initiative creates a powerful opportunity for you to engage with your customers to share the costs, grow revenue and do more good. By strategically considering the best way to engage your particular customers with your particular products and services, you can create three-way victory for the company, the customer and the cause.

Chapter 6

Building a Bottom-up Movement

IN THE MID-1980S, while polio was only a generational memory in the U.S., it remained a global epidemic, with 350,000 to 400,000 cases reported each year. In 2015, there were about 70 cases of polio reported in the entire world. A reported 20 million health care workers and volunteers were engaged in fighting polio. This movement will almost certainly celebrate the last and final case of polio in 2016 and the world will be free from this disease forever.

For the past three years, I have been studying the growth of this movement to understand how it works so that we can replicate the success in addressing other global problems. These lessons apply perfectly to the process of building a purpose program at your company from the grass roots.

In order to understand the polio eradication movement, let's look at a few details.

The movement began with a Rotary Club in Australia that traveled to the Philippines to vaccinate children there. Soon, other

Rotary Clubs joined in and the movement was born. What started the movement? The answer is simple: action. A few Rotarians actually went to the Philippines and started vaccinating kids.

The next phase of the effort involved Rotary International. The global group decided to make polio eradication a formal goal of the organization. It raised $250 million to start the global effort and recruited partners, including the U.S. Centers for Disease Control and UNICEF. Over the years, the World Health Organization, the Bill and Melinda Gates Foundation and governments around the world joined the fight.

By the early aughts of this century, the number of polio cases had fallen to fewer than 1,000 per year, representing more than a 99 percent reduction in cases of polio. Only four countries were still considered endemic, never having eradicated the disease within their borders: Pakistan, Afghanistan, India and Nigeria. For nearly a decade, however, the number of cases didn't decline further.

The Global Polio Eradication Initiative led by Rotary International realized that an "end game strategy" would be required to complete the job. The world couldn't simply keep on doing what it was doing and expect to eradicate the disease. Budgets were tripled with massive help from the Gates Foundation, Rotarians around the world, governments and others. With the increased funding, came more focus on the few remaining hot spots and they began to drop off. The last case of polio in India was in 2011. The last case in Nigeria came in 2014 and as of this writing, only Pakistan and Afghanistan are still considered endemic. Even in these countries, catching a wild case of polio is rare. The last case of polio could easily be reported within the next 90 days.

So the movement to eradicate polio has three observable phases:

1. Start taking action

2. Build support and momentum

3. End game strategy

Let's apply this to your grass-roots effort to build a CSR program in your organization.

The first step is to start doing something yourself or with a small group of employees. At this point, you should be tackling something that aligns well with the corporate mission and that won't require a budget or much formal permission.

Let's consider an effort to develop a zero waste policy beginning with the accounting department. Rather than push the boss to impose a zero waste policy on the group, adopt your own zero waste policy.

There are really three key steps for the first phase of a grass-roots program.

First, focus on execution over elegance. In the example of a zero waste policy, you'll probably want to begin by recycling everything that can be recycled. This may require sorting and separating. You may need several containers in your cube. Rather than buy a commercial recycling sorter, grab three cardboard boxes from the copy room as reams of paper get used for printing reports each day. Not elegant, but fully functional.

Second, you need to prove that it works. There are plenty of offices that separate their recyclable materials into various containers only to have the cleaning staff come by at the end of the day and toss everything into the garbage headed for the landfill. If you're going to create a zero waste department, you better make sure that what you separate for recycling is actually getting recycled. Make a few calls to find out how the waste streams are handled and if necessary, make arrangements for special handling. It may be that recycling paper is working flawlessly, but electronics and the hazardous wastes from the printers in the office may be going to the landfill. Find a way to get those items recycled. Prove that you can be a zero waste office.

Third, you'll want to make and measure progress. Assuming that you are working all alone, be sure to track the impact of your effort to create a zero waste policy for your cubicle. You may find that over the course of a single month, you recycle hundreds of pounds of paper and plastic and, perhaps more importantly, you've redirected some of the most toxic waste from the accounting department into appropriate recycling programs. Be sure to look for savings and profits in your tracking. Did you reduce your use of paper, toner and ink? How much did that save? Measure your progress and report it.

Now you are ready for the second phase of the grass roots effort at CSR: build support.

First, you'll want to recruit some colleagues to join your effort. In any large accounting department, it shouldn't be hard to find a few who are as interested in the environment and company profits as you are. In fact, if anything you've been doing is visible, everyone in the department is probably talking about you already. You may not have to recruit so much as train. Show your friends how to replicate what you're doing. They may have good ideas for improving the zero waste campaign, too.

Second, at this point, you may want or need to get some formal sanction or approval for the program. You'll know best, but note that by getting "official" approval for your "pilot program" you make it easier and more comfortable for people to join you.

Third, with the formal approval for the program you may want or need a modest budget. If you can demonstrate that your program could save more money than the budget you are requesting, you can begin building the case for your program. This may give you an opportunity to replace cardboard boxes in your cubical with sorted recycling bins in the office.

It may require months or years of tracking and reporting progress, recruiting new members of the department to your cause and piles of evidence to convince the higher ups to mandate the program you've built on a volunteer basis. Keep it up. Recognize, however, that you won't likely get the mandate you are looking for without some controversy.

With the progress you have made to this point, it may be time to develop your end game strategy to get the entire accounting department on board with your program. You will probably need a mandate from the department head to make the program into official policy.

First, you need to be prepared for opposition. If you've been running your volunteer zero-waste program long enough, you've probably involved everyone who is willing to participate without a mandate. While some of those who haven't volunteered, will be willing to go along without complaint if required, some will become outspoken critics. You may know who they are already. They be teasing or even bullying you, pouring coffee in your paper recycling bins and such. If you push for a policy, you can bet they will push back.

Note, too, that other problems may arise. You may find that it is virtually free to recycle electronic waste for one person or for three people, but you may need to pay to have a full department's electronic waste recycled. Such news could break the budget and crash the model you've built to make your case. You need to plan and prepare for all of these possible challenges. Creating a zero waste department won't be easy, even after you've proven to yourself and your like-minded colleagues that it works.

Second, you'll need to get the department head to give you the mandate or policy you're asking for. In the polio battle, it became clear that no amount of volunteering would work to eradicate polio without the support of local and national governments. Your department won't truly be operating on a zero waste basis until it is the formal policy. Make your case.

Third, and finally, you'll need more of a budget. If you've created a proper CSR program, you'll be able to demonstrate cost savings or revenues that will fully offset the costs of the program, but that doesn't mean the program won't have costs. Be prepared to defend the need for the program. One of the challenges you may face is that your waste handling budget may simply be an allocation of the company's total waste handling budget. In other words, the benefit you are creating in the accounting department may not be reflected in the accounting department's budget. On the other hand, if you need a budget to run the program, that will almost certainly be in the department budget. Be prepared to defend the budget requirement in that circumstance. Either work to change the budget allocations so both the costs and benefits are reflected within your department or help higher ups to see and measure the benefits even if they aren't reflected in the budget.

Remember, I've used this vaguely defined zero-waste initiative as a loose example to help you see how you can build a purpose program from the bottom up. You can apply the same principles to tutoring children at the nearby elementary school, feeding the homeless or caring for seniors living on fixed incomes. Find the intersection between your passion for good in the world and the company's mission and find a way to take action.

Chapter 7

Messaging Your Mission

REMEMBER, I SEE this world through the prism of my experience as a new media journalist and a former CFO and investment banker. While your messaging around your purpose program is incredibly important, you'll want to work closely with real marketing professionals to develop your program. I hope the following insights are instructive.

Develop a Strategy

While it is always important to have a clear branding and marketing strategy, the potential for doing harm to your brand is even greater with your purpose program than when you are promoting your products and services. If you don't create an honest impression of being authentically engaged in solving a problem of adequate scale for your organization, you run the risk of setting your organization up for social media ridicule rather than praise. To put this in clear language a CFO will understand, if you are thinking about spending more money bragging about your impact than you spent creating that impact, you know you're in trouble.

There are three basic principles to keep in mind when developing your message around your cause.

First, minimize the traditional advertising. In general, people will respond skeptically to self-reported good deeds. Even the most genuinely created and effective impact programs can fail in the messaging when you are the messenger. Advertising can be most effective when you are calling on your customers to join you in the effort. In that case, the audience understands that the purpose of the message is a call to arms and not a boast.

Second, incorporate professional public relations. If you haven't had a professional public relations effort up to this point—and some small businesses don't—the completion of a project for the community creates the perfect opportunity to spend a few dollars here. In the new media jungle, it has never been more challenging to get press, but good press has never been more important or more valuable. Social media gives you a tool for sharing positive press with your customers and employees—and for them to share it with their friends, meaning that the ripples from the media are potentially larger than ever before.

Third, as implied by the last point, you need to strategically incorporate social media into your campaign. It is likely that Facebook, Twitter and Instagram will be the keys to your reaching your community, but as new platforms are launched every day, it is possible if not likely that as you read this, you'll need to be focusing somewhere else as well. It isn't enough to have social media accounts; you'll have to learn to engage with your community online in an authentic way. One key part of that is sharing your CSR efforts with them via social media.

The three elements of your plan can and should work synergistically (please forgive the 90s buzz word, but it works here) together. Here's what I mean. Let's say that your PR team generates a great story in the *Huffington Post*. A typical post there likely will get 1,000 to 10,000 views (some get many, many more, but they aren't typical). If you share it on social media to your community, many of the people you care most about seeing it, will. To reach virtually all of them and to reach some new prospects as well, you may need to pay for some advertising on social media. If you are spending $5,000 on public relations, it makes sense to spend another $500 on social media advertising to ensure that water reaches the end of the row (a big concern for farmers out west here where I was raised because crops are watered not by rain but by irrigation).

Combine Action and Communication

Increasingly, technology will allow you to help your community to share what they are doing in the instant they do it. This is relatively easy when your customers donate online or make a purchase with proceeds going to a cause on your site. You can enable a tweet or a Facebook post immediately after or perhaps even concurrent with making the donation or purchase.

Consider the New Belgium Brewing glasses as an example. At the moment that a customer completes the purchase, the customer could be prompted with a pre-populated tweet or Facebook post or an Instagram photo with an appropriate caption ready to share. The post could note the purchase with a photo and the cause to which the buyer directed the donation.

The post should include two hashtags as well. One should be a common hashtag that connects the post to an ongoing dialog, say #love or #service. The other hashtag should be unique to your company or even unique to the campaign. For instance, Chevron runs a program each year called Fuel Your School to raise money for teachers in communities where Chevron has a large presence. The hashtag #fuelyourschool could be used along with the hashtag #education to maximize social media impact. The unique hashtag connects all of the posts about the program together while the broad hashtag connects the post to a larger community of people who follow #education.

Of course, not all customers will post to social media, but when you consider that those who do have the potential to reach hundreds if not thousands of friends with a single post, helping your customers share at that moment of giving should be a top priority in your messaging strategy.

Empower Your Community to Share the Message

While it is likely to backfire if you try to force employees or customers to engage with you on social media, the easier you make it the more likely they are to do it.

Writing a 140 character, that is tweet-length message, is challenging for clever professionals; writing interesting tweets that you'll be glad to have shared, is even more challenging for your community members. They may be perfectly willing to brag about their donation to a favorite cause through your company, but finding the right words, incorporating a link they've now forgotten, finding the right photo to accompany it and then choosing a hashtag is quite reasonably too much to ask.

In order to overcome this challenge, you'll want to create templates that your community can share easily. You can certainly post these from your own account and hope that they get retweeted and shared. You may also want to include sharing buttons with these pre-populated messages on your blog, your website and your email newsletter. You could even include a QR code in printed mailings that would help your customers share their participation in your purpose program on social media.

Don't forget to engage those you serve in your communication strategy. Many will be willing to participate in one way or another, even if it is just to tweet a thank you. If you're helping a population without Twitter accounts, say sea turtles or preschoolers, remember that there are people interfacing between you and them who do have the ability to tweet. Some organizations, in fact, have large communication departments and resources and may be eager to engage with you in planning your public relations and social media campaigns. And, of course, you can mention the organizations you support in your advertising.

Chapter 8

Hold Yourself Accountable

YOUR PRIMARY GOAL is to increase the profit of your firm. You've learned that one of the keys to increasing profit with a corporate social responsibility program is to be authentic, to actually find a cause you and your organization can genuinely support in hopes of making a measurable impact on the problem. Therefore, you've got to measure the profit impacts and your social impact in order to determine if what you're doing is actually working.

Analyze the Profit Impact:

Even those who tell me they are confident their CSR programs increase their companies bottom line, have difficulty quantifying the numbers. The costs are typically easy to measure. Please measure them. You can't determine the profit without calculating the costs! The benefits are typically more difficult to measure. Some programs where firms create a specific product to be sold for social impact purposes can track the revenue and expenses associated with that product and determine the profitability of that product,

DEVIN D. THORPE

but the benefits to the company may be larger than the profits on that line.

A good CSR program will enhance the revenue of the company across the board. How much of revenue growth (or in a down year, how much of revenue retained) can be attributed to the purpose program is difficult—perhaps impossible—to measure. That doesn't mean you shouldn't make an effort with your brightest people to evaluate revenue impacts.

You'll also want to look at direct cost savings. Some programs, like the hypothetical zero-waste program we discussed in Chapter 6, will drive direct, measurable costs savings. They may not be easy to track, but you should be able to measure before and after differences to understand how much money you are saving if direct cost savings were a goal.

You'll also want to look for indirect savings and productivity gains. Again, these can be hard to measure, but you may be able to draw conclusions by comparing costs and productivity before and after the implementation of the program. If the program causes ten percent of your employees to become more engaged, that benefit should show up on the bottom line. Your challenge is to find it.

One way to make measurement of profits easier is to establish careful measurements of revenue and expense levels that may be impacted by the program before you launch it. If you predict the financial impacts carefully on a line-by-line basis, you'll have an easier time measuring them after the fact.

Evaluate the Social Impact:

To determine the impact of your CSR program, you'll have to start by measuring your activities, but you can't stop there. What you do, time spent training employees, the time you all spend volunteering for the cause and the checks you write in support of the cause are all part of the activities you should be tracking and reporting. Imagine reporting that your team donated 100 hours, 1,000 hours or 100,000 hours of their time to your cause. If you have enough people, those numbers are achievable. A firm with 5,000 employees who all volunteer an average of 20 hours in a year would have volunteered 100,000 hours! That's only about 1 percent of their time. And don't forget to measure the money you've donated, whether that comes out of your profits or is gathered from your employees and customers, tally it up.

Don't stop there. Your activities really aren't the goal. Whether you are working toward helping the poor, the uneducated, the environment or whatever, your goal really isn't to volunteer and give money, it is to have impact. Look past the activities to the impact. In some cases, this can be as difficult as measuring the profitability.

If you are volunteering with and/or giving money to a nonprofit partner for your purpose program, you can and should ask the partner to help you measure impact. They may start with measuring your inputs into their program, again as volunteer hours and dollars, but they are also likely tracking people served, trees planted, animals rescued, etc. They can help translate your activities into first order outcomes relatively easily.

Ultimately, you want to go even further in the analysis, to look past the activities and outcomes to the real impact. For instance, if you are volunteering time tutoring kids, it is easy to track the volunteer hours (activity) and outcomes (students tutored) but what we are most interested in are the impacts of the tutoring. Did grades improve? Did at-risk students stay in school rather than drop out at a higher rate than before the tutoring began? Did more students advance to the next grade? Did more students go on to college? Are more students taking STEM (science, technology, engineering and math) electives? Are the students happier and more success-ful? How else can you measure impact?

What you measure and how you measure it will depend on the cause you tackle and the goals you set. Don't be afraid to measure for impacts outside your goals. You might set a goal to increase graduation rates and you may even measure success with that ob-jective. Might you also find that you increased college enrollments? Could it be that you've reduced drug use among at-risk students? There may be any number of benefits you could measure in addi-tion to the one you chose at the outset.

Ask Your Community

It is also a good idea to ask your employees and customers how they feel about the company and the program after it is well un-derway. Depending on the size of the company, you may not feel a need to ask all of your employees or all of your customers, but you'll want to at least ask some.

Microsoft reported in its annual corporate citizenship report that 90 percent of employees say they are proud to work at Mic-rosoft. Obviously, that pride is influence by many factors, including the success of the business and the work of the Bill and Melinda Gates Foundation, which is completely independent of the CSR ef-forts at Microsoft, but some may be tied to the company's purpose programs. Microsoft awards cash grants to nonprofits totaling over $100 million and donates its products and services to the tune of nearly $1 billion annually. That would make me proud to work at Microsoft.

As you look to find the profit from your purpose program, be sure to balance your effort in finding the social impact you've had. The great thing about corporate giving is that it can go on forever. While people live and die and employees come and go, your company can literally live indefinitely. Be patient with yourself in finding the profit and the social impact. If you can't find the profit the first year but you see great social impact, look for ways to share more of the costs with customers and employees. If you are profitable, but don't see the social impact you're seeking, tweak or pivot your purpose program as may be needed to drive more impact next year.

Once you have the profit and the impact dialed in, you can scale your program as you grow your business and the profit and impact of your program can truly become infinite.

Chapter 9

You Can Change the World

ALL BUT THE most cynical CFOs who read this book, will feel a bit of unease over the idea that corporations should add purpose programs solely to increase their own profitability. Let's consider that for a moment.

Attitudes and mores around personal social responsibility vary significantly from person to person and culture to culture. One evidence of this is that even between states in the U.S., the percentage of incomes donated to charity vary dramatically.

Even with all of that diversity, most people feel that giving should be motivated by a desire to help rather than by a selfish interest like increasing profit. That is exactly why I've emphasized the need for a CSR program to be authentic, starting with finding something that the people in your organization can or do care about.

Wanting your program to improve profitability isn't just practical, it is noble. If your purpose program doesn't enhance profitability, it will be limited in scale to that which management, share-holders and the board of directors can tolerate as a tax on profits.

On the other hand, if the purpose program enhances profitability, the scale of the good you do can, as I've noted before, be infinite.

When I was a CFO, the President, Dell Brown, of the company taught me an important principle that he'd learned from the nuns running a Catholic Hospital where he'd done some consulting. Their mantra, "no margin, no mission" made clear that without profitability they couldn't treat patients. Whatever your cause may be, we recognize that if serving that cause isn't ultimately profitable for the company there is little you can do for it.

Be assured that your purpose program will make a difference in the world if you are as thoughtful and strategic about the program as you are with the rest of the business. There are on the order of 5 billion people living on less than $10 per day and fully a billion of them live on less than $2 per day and are considered to be experiencing extreme poverty. Homelessness is a problem that seems to afflict every city in the world. The environment is facing a long list of challenges as well, many of which can be observed right in your own community. Whatever you choose to tackle, there is an opportunity for you to make a difference.

The collective effort of thousands of companies engaging meaningfully and passionately in solving problems at a scale appropriate to their size will make a huge collective difference. When Coke and Pepsi began working in earnest to protect natural water resources nearly a decade ago, it was hard to imagine the impact they'd have. The Nature Conservancy's CEO, Mark Tercek, has touted their work in his book *Nature's Fortune*. By doing so, they have avoided some of the angry attention that Nestle has received over its water use.

We are living at an amazing moment in history. Most of us will leave to see the Earth's population peak and begin to stabilize, not because of war or famine, but because of global prosperity. Affluent people simply don't have as many children as poor ones do. That world of 9 or 10 billion relatively affluent people will likely consume vastly more of what your company sells. There are threats to that picture, but business has never been better situated to help create the sustainable, egalitarian world in which everyone has the opportunity to prosper.

Chapter 10

M·A·C AIDS Fund Case Study

ESTÉE LAUDER'S M·A·C Cosmetics brand years ago established the M·A·C AIDS Fund, a nonprofit organization funded by M·A·C Cosmetics to fight HIV/AIDS. It is certainly the most impactful CSR program I have ever seen, both as seen from the standpoint of enhancing profits and as measured by its impact on AIDS.

As of 2016, since 1994, over $412 million has been raised to fight AIDS. In 2014, a total of $48 million was raised and the tally was expected to be even bigger in 2015. This is an almost incredible scale. The only companies that have donated more to any cause, according to my research, are much larger than Estée Lauder.

Over the past few years, I have had the opportunity to visit with Nancy Mahon, Estée Lauder's Senior Vice President, Global Philanthropy and Corporate Citizenship, on my YouTube show on two occasions. She has assured me that this program that contributed $48 million to charity in a single year is profitable.

Let's look briefly at how that works. M·A·C Cosmetics uses a version of the product proceeds model of CSR program, where a single product, in this case Viva Glam lipstick, is devoted to a cause. So, when a retailer sells a Viva Glam lipstick from M·A·C Cosmetics, 100 percent of the sales price goes to the M·A·C AIDS Fund. As of 2016, the price for Viva Glam lipstick is $17. That entire amount is donated to the fund for every sale. Much of the lipstick is sold from company-owned stores. When department stores sell Viva Glam lipstick—and they are required by M·A·C Cosmetics to do so in order to carry the M·A·C line—they share their margin on the product as well.

M·A·C Cosmetics still has to produce and distribute the product—it doesn't magically appear on store shelves. M·A·C absorbs those costs as part of its contribution to the M·A·C AIDS Fund. Nancy insists that Estée Lauder is more profitable as a result of this program, despite its costs.

The profits, she says, come from several places, including the incredible value of having people engaged with purpose throughout the entire company.

M·A·C Cosmetics also get a benefit from a tradeoff between their M·A·C AIDS Fund expenses and the industry standard of providing expensive gifts with a purchase. If you've ever purchased other department store brands, you know that purchases often come with a gift pack of expensive samples of other brand products. M·A·C Cosmetics doesn't do that. Instead, they communicate that customers are getting "good" with their purchase instead of a gift with purchase.

Another key to the financial success of the program is the spokeswomen who market the products. Because of the authentic, impactful programs at M·A·C Cosmetics, women including

Lady Gaga, Rihanna and Miley Cyrus have all signed on to pro-mote the products. Not only have they been willing to do this, but Mahon says they have done it generously, working for a fraction of their market value, because they want to be associated with fight-ing AIDS. Pitching Viva Glam gives them a genuine connection to the cause. Big names are lining up for the opportunity, accelerating the success of Viva Glam.

The M·A·C AIDS Fund is the second largest private funder of the fight against HIV/AIDS following only the Bill and Melinda Gates Foundation, Mahon says. This provides a remarkable syner-gy. Mahon herself and her colleagues are invited to be a part of the discussion when the global leaders in the fight against HIV/AIDS gather. Mahon and her colleagues bring something to the table that most of the others do not. They bring marketing savvy.

Think about how this leverages the impact of the M·A·C AIDS Fund financial contributions. By providing marketing expertise as well, their money does more good. They are actually adding more value than the money alone might bring. That also reflects back on M·A·C Cosmetics, enhancing the value of the brand as the impact of their contribution is expanded. A truly virtuous cycle is created by the contribution of money and expertise, as the impact increas-es, so does their influence and the reflected brand value.

When the fight against HIV/AIDS is won, I like to think that M·A·C Cosmetics will host the after party. Lots of people will be invited to that party. The GATES Foundation and the Global Fund will certainly receive special recognition and countless others will deserve thanks, but M·A·C Cosmetics alone brings the glam to a party that will be celebrated around the world.

While you may be tempted to doubt that this is even possi-ble, don't. Experts in the field are exultant that a vaccine could be ready within a few short years. The eradication of small pox (1980) and polio (~2019) makes clear that we can eradicate HIV/AIDS once we have a vaccine. And Estée Lauder's M·A·C Cosmetics brand will have played a critical part.

The dollars involved in this example may be daunting to you and your organization. Please, don't let the scale scare you. Let this example inspire you. If you are the CFO for a relatively small business, you're not going to drive impact of this magnitude, but that doesn't mean that you can't drive impact at a meaningful scale. Match the scale of your program to the scale of your company. Your impact may be local, but even local challenges are manifestations of global problems. You'll be doing your part. You can make a difference that will make a difference to your company, too.

Conclusion

The Power of Profit to Drive Impact

TODAY, I WORK as a journalist to advocate for doing good, but I remember my days as a CFO and the influence that I had then. I miss the power and influence I had back then. The scale of our business and profits gave me an opportunity to write bigger checks than I can imagine doing personally today.

You are now where I was. have the power and influence I once had. I hope this book will inspire you to solve a social problem in your community or the world—and do so profitably.

As a CFO, you are in a powerful position to make the sort of changes I'm talking about. Often, others in the company will believe the principles of this book before you're convinced. They may fear coming to you for support, fearing reasonably that any idea advocating for using corporate resources to advance a social cause will be shot down. Prove them wrong.

Prove to yourself and the company that by strategically partnering with employees and customers, you can create a purpose program with significant impact that is profitable. Before you launch, establish measurement protocols for both profitability and impact. Play your role well. Be merciless for the sake of the program. Find a way to make it profitable so no one can ever shut it down.

Remember that if you create a program that doesn't increase the profit of the organization overall, its impact is limited. It will be difficult for you to justify any expansion. Shareholders may complain, especially if the impact of the effort is questionable. Such programs are destined for to be kicked to the curb.

On the other hand, if you can create an authentic, effective program that captures the hearts and minds of employees and customers alike, it can have a transformative impact on the company, growing profits and driving impact at an unlimited scale. If it is increasing your profits, are you going to argue for shutting it down? Of course not! Not only can it continue, it can and should grow with the scale of the company as it grows.

You can lead the creation of impact without limitation and accelerate profits at the same time. No matter how big your company is today and regardless of the scale on which it may do good this year, companies can outlive people and they can grow to enormous size and influence. Imagine how much good your company can do over the next 20 years if the good you do increases your revenue and profitability. Imagine the good it will do over the next 50 years, 100 years if you help build that focus into the company's mission and values.

Some of the world's biggest problems can be overcome entirely with systematic effort across time. You can take pride in knowing that you got the ball rolling in your company, a ball that might one day play a pivotal role in the eradication of disease, the education of billions or the protection of the environment upon which we and future generations depend for life.

On every episode of my show, now approaching 700 episodes, I sign off with a challenge to my guests, my audience and myself. "Let's do some good!" I promise that if you do it right, you'll not only do a lot of good, you'll do well for yourself and your company as you do.

Appendix

Why CSR? The Benefits of Corporate Social Responsibility Will Move You to Act

THIS ARTICLE WAS originally published on Forbes.com *on May 18, 2013 and has become the most popular article I've written for* Forbes. *I share it here as reference.*

Recently, I connected with dozens of corporate executives of large and small companies in an effort to understand the benefits of corporate social responsibility (CSR) to the corporation.

The question, I learned, is harder to answer than you might expect, principally because most corporate do-gooders approach their social good efforts with more of an eye toward impact on the community than on the firm.

With some effort, however, I've pulled some meaningful responses from corporate leaders I've reached and learned a great deal in the process.

Garratt Hasenstab,
Director of Sustainability at the Verdigris Group,
courtesy of the Verdigis Group

Garratt Hasenstab, Director of Sustainability at the Verdigris Group, a real estate development and consulting firm, says, "Verdigris Group is focused on being a leader in the area of corporate social responsibility. We have developed and established a comprehensive set of sustainable business initiatives that facilitate our triple bottom-line approach to operating our business." He notes that the firm has operated "as a certified carbon-neutral business since 2007." The firm engages its employees actively in all of its sustainability initiatives.

Hasenstab adds, "Verdigris Group is fortunate to work with some of the most socially and environmentally conscious clients and partners in our industry. Those that we work with, both partner companies and clients alike are actively engaged in our sustainability efforts and take pride in being involved with a company that is focused on the triple bottom-line of people, planet, profit."

He concludes by saying, "Our CSR policy is at the core of our daily operations and guides our future progress. We benefit from these efforts in a number of ways. Our clients want to work with us because we are focused on a healthier and more productive world. Our development clients can rely on us to develop their projects to the highest standards of energy efficiency and occupant health, while creating an architecturally resonant project that reflects our mission and vision. Of course we save money by operating more efficiently which is a direct benefit of our CSR efforts, however the true value we receive from our ongoing initiatives is that of social good will - we believe that setting a good example is the greatest benefit in that we inspire other organizations, companies and individuals to ‹up their game› when it comes to social and environmental responsibility, which in turn encourages further inspiration in the community leading to a more enlightened perspective on how to run one's business or lead one's life."

While each company I interviewed had varying responses for the benefits of CSR and cause marketing for the company, 51 of 59 believe that they have happier employees and 45 of the 59 believe they end up with better employees, either as a result of being able to attract better talent or that the CSR programs help to develop better employees.

John G. Taft,
great-grandson of President Taft and CEO
of RBC Wealth Management-USA, courtesy of RBC

John G. Taft, great-grandson of President Taft and CEO of RBC Wealth Management-USA, which reports $227 billion of assets under management, describes one of their CSR initiatives, "The RBC Blue Water Project is a 10-year global commitment to help protect the world's most precious natural resource: fresh water. It includes a $50 million philanthropic commitment to organizations that protect watersheds and ensure access to clean drinking water." He notes that "Clients are often invited to participate in RBC sponsored local events with nonprofits."

Taft further explains, "For the sixth year, RBC employees around the globe will participate in Blue Water Day on June 14. On this day, employees will volunteer their time to participate in a Community Makeover with a local nonprofit to help preserve fresh water in urban areas." He adds, "I have personally attended Blue Water Day activities and have seen firsthand the commitment of our employees to the environment. Last year, in Minneapolis, we cleared invasive species from a local riverbank so the natural vegetation can thrive and be a natural filter for runoff that flows into the river. The demonstrated commitment by the company and employees makes me proud to work for RBC." He sums up the benefits to the company this way, "Employees and customers want to work with a company that they respect."

Lisa Dewey,
DLA Piper Pro Bono Partner; Director, New Perimeter,
courtesy of DLA Piper

Similarly, Lisa Dewey, Pro Bono Partner at DLA Piper, one of the world's largest law firms, says the firm "is deeply committed to Corporate Responsibility initiatives through pro bono service, community engagement, diversity and environmental sustainability." She further explains, "In the United States, DLA Piper structures its pro bono program around "Signature Projects," which are designed to commit significant resources to tackling major social issues, including education, hunger relief, juvenile justice, access to justice, domestic violence and serving veterans. DLA Piper's signature projects are often developed in partnership with nonprofit organizations, academic institutions, foundations and the firm's corporate clients." She adds, "Globally, New Perimeter, a nonprofit organization established by DLA Piper in 2005, provides pro bono legal assistance primarily in developing and post-conflict regions."

When asked about the involvement of employees, she responded, "All DLA Piper attorneys and staff are encouraged to participate in the firm's pro bono and volunteer projects. The wide scope of our pro bono program allows employees to choose causes that are important to them and provides several options for giving back to their communities and helping those less fortunate. I continue to be astounded by the tireless dedication of our attorneys to pro bono service and to projects that often span multiple years and require substantial time commitment and cross-border travel."

As to the benefit to the firm, she comments, "The success of our pro bono programs and the unwavering commitment of our lawyers has truly made a difference in the lives of others both in the U.S. and globally, and has made us all better lawyers and DLA Piper a better firm." She also noted, "DLA Piper's deep commitment to pro bono and CSR initiatives has had a positive impact on the firm, its attorneys and staff, and clients across numerous areas. We've seen a noticeable impact in terms of strengthening relationships with clients, providing young attorneys practical and hands-on experience, improving employee morale, and deepening the firm's ties to the many communities in which it operates."

Shaun Walker, the Creative Director and Co-Founder of HEROfarm, a marketing agency in New Orleans, explained their approach to CSR, saying, "A cornerstone of HEROfarm is to do at least one pro bono campaign per year (often doing much more) for a non-profit, as well as work with clients who have admirable missions of their own." Walker reports that the firm has supported organizations as varied as the American Cancer Society, Boy Scouts of America and Tulane University's media arts program. He notes, "True success comes when everyone focuses on the bigger picture and here, the bigger picture isn't just about doing your job—it's about trying to change the world for the better." This spirit carries over to client relationships, he adds, "An old saying goes,

'In seeking happiness for others, you find it for yourself.' We truly believe that. People remember the kindness and smiles you share with them and how you made them feel, not what kind of car you drove or what designer clothing you wore."

HEROfarm, says Walker, has received numerous awards and other accolades which he attributes to the pro bono work the firm does, "We also measure these results by our rising name recognition, as seen by our increasing accolades as we've matured, and by the fact our revenue has risen every year since our founding four years ago."

Gary Beu,
Managing Director of People and Leadership Development
at West Monroe Partners, courtesy of West Monroe Partners

In another example, Gary Beu, Managing Director of People and Leadership Development at the consulting firm West Monroe Partners, says, "At the end of 2011, West Monroe Partners launched its "1+1+1 Program," a corporate social responsibility initiative through which we would donate 1 percent of our time, 1-percent of our treasure and 1-percent of our talent, each year, back to organizations in our communities." He adds, "Since kicking off our 1+1+1 Program, West Monroe Partners has collectively matched 1,500 employee volunteer hours, completed nearly 4,000 hours for pro bono projects across the United States, and donated over $250,000 to non-profit organizations."

Beu goes on to say, "Our 1+1+1 Program empowers our employees to give back to our communities in a way that complements their personal and professional lives." When pressed for the benefits to the company, Beu responds, "The goals that we set through our volunteer initiatives have given us an even deeper sense of purpose and motivation to do the best work possible in and outside of the office. West Monroe Partners has always been a community of driven, creative and curious people, but our social good efforts especially have brought out the compassion and loyalty in all of us."

Joe Mechlinski, CEO of the Baltimore-based consulting firm entreQuest and author of Grow Regardless with whom I did a live interview recently, sees "giving back to the community" as "an essential key to a successful business because it not only lifts morale and builds capability among the team, but it also clears people's minds allowing them to make better decisions." The eQ team conducts "Give Back Days" where the employees serve meals at Our Daily Bread, a local soup kitchen, work with Habitat for Humanity on local housing, mentor children through b4Students and Big Brothers Big Sisters and more.

For Mechlinski, social good goes beyond his own company. He says, "We encourage all of our clients to find a cause (or causes) meaningful to them and help them coordinate Give Back Days for their entire team. In fact, we believe in the power of these Give Back Days so much so that we typically recommend a Give Back Day as part of a two-day strategy retreat—on the first day the company has a Give Back Day where they focus on serving others and feeding their souls, then on the second day they are more ready to work through tough strategy decisions in order to cultivate an environment of growth, align their team, and positively impact both the employee and client experience."

Mechlinski says the evidence that their community focus pays off is in their recognition two years in a row as one of Baltimore's Best Places to Work. He also noted, "I was honored to be named one of Maryland's Most Admired CEO's by The Daily Record last year. Again, much of what determined this award was the fact that as a leader, I've made it a priority to give back to my community and encourage my team to do the same."

Some businesses are built from the ground up to do social good; these social enterprises are wired differently, says Soapbox CEO and Co-founder, David Simnick, "Soapbox Soaps started with the idea that a simple bar of soap could legitimately save kids' lives. We've now grown into offering a line of health and beauty products that have a mission attached to each one. The grand idea is to empower customers with the ability to change the world through simple, every day purchases. For example, every bottle of our liquid hand soap buys one month of clean water to a child in need through RainCatcher."

Simnick points out that for Soapbox, the mission came first, "We started the company first because we wanted to stop child mortality due to lack of access to hygiene. We only figured out how to sell soap afterwards." He adds, "Without the social mission, our company would not exist."

Shel Horowitz, a CSR consultant who says he practices what he preaches, says, "For the past ten years or so, I've been very publicly touting the benefits of eco/social responsibility—in my books, articles, blog, and speeches. I don't think it's a coincidence that during this period, my business underwent significant growth in average per-client revenue and total revenue."

While some can quickly identify the benefits of their CSR initiatives, others can't see past the benefit to others to measure the benefits for their own firms.

John Paul Engel,
President of Knowledge Capital Consulting,
courtesy of Knowledge Capital Consulting

John Paul Engel, President of Knowledge Capital Consulting, which launched Project Be The Change (PBTC) to provide help in a variety of forms. In a remarkable observation, Engel notes that most of their employees started as volunteers in their PBTC. When asked about the benefits to the company, he responded, "Everyone gets excited when we have a successful project. I think it makes everyone feel good that our work is paid forward and that we are positively impacting so many people beyond our clients."

Tara Wilson, the principal attorney at Wilson, LF, a "boutique" law firm with offices in Andover Massachusetts and Washington, DC, has made community service and pro bono work a central part of the firm's strategy. She believes this has led to having "a higher profile in the communities we serve because they recognize our firm from our charitable endeavors."

Examples of CSR program are as varied as the companies that sponsor them.

Karen Ross, CEO of Sharp Decisions, an IT consultancy that supports government clients, describes their V.E.T.S. Program (Vocations, Education and Training for Service members), which helps veterans of the Iraq and Afghanistan wars to find jobs. Retention is improved, she says, by sending the candidates out in "squads." Ross sees the benefits of the new program already, reporting, "We have had an outpouring of response and support from our current clients, some who have their own veteran outreach initiatives. Many of the companies we work with have been very receptive to our ideas about training and rightshoring jobs for these heroes. The V.E.T.S. Program adds a different dimension to the Sharp Decisions story, and that resonates with many of our prospective clients as well."

Some companies observe that their employees develop new skills and abilities through their nonprofit service.

Ryan McEvoy,
a Principal at California-based Gaia Development,
courtesy of Gaia Development

Ryan McEvoy, a Principal at California-based Gaia Development, which does sustainable development, helped found Collective Solutions, a nonprofit organization that is confronting poverty and climate change. A percentage of Gaia's revenue is donated to Collective Solutions each year, he says, and notes that "Employees are encouraged to dedicate their time and expertise to something beyond the realm of day-to-day business, and many find that outlet in Collective Solutions." Employees recently participated in a trip to Nicaragua where they helped families learn to build effective solar ovens from scrap materials including cardboard to reduce their dependence on declining supplies of wood.

Of the benefits to Gaia, McEvoy notes, "Collective Solutions offers our employees a chance to think-outside-of-the-box and apply their years of experience and advanced skills in new ways. Our employees, who traveled with us to El Carizal, show remarkable versatility and creativity. They know how to seek out the simplest solutions (ovens out of cardboard?), which are oftentimes the most effective."

Art Papas,
founder and CEO of Bullhorn, courtesy of Bullhorn

Art Papas, founder and CEO of Bullhorn, a software company serving recruiters, says, "Bullhorn's corporate mission is to help recruiters put the world to work. Our employees volunteer their time and we make donations to organizations that seek to end working class poverty like Career Collaborative and Youth Villages. And all of the charities we support aim to help the community at large and prepare individuals for a more productive life." He is obviously proud of the extent to which employees are involved, "Each employee receives a day off per quarter to do community service and volunteer. The Bullhorn Cares committee – a team of individuals that organizes, plans and markets these various events to the rest of the company – actively recruits employees from across Bullhorn to volunteer time, money, and effort to help with a variety of community service initiatives."

Among the benefits he observes, "Customers appreciate Bullhorn employees' dedication to service, as it shows through not just in how we help the less fortunate but also in how we respect everyone around us. Bullhorn excels at both customer service and community service." He adds, "These efforts demonstrate to employees that we share their personal values. It changes the employment relationship—it's not just about a pay check, it's about working together to accomplish something."

Tyler Collins,
CEO of Orange County SEO, courtesy of Orange County SEO

Likewise, Tyler Collins, CEO of Orange County SEO, of California, says, "Orange County SEO offers charities and philanthropies free search engine optimization and online marketing." He notes, "Every employee is actively engaged in Orange County SEO's social good efforts. We all work together as a team to promote our charitable clients through search engine optimization, public relations, and social media. Employees gain a sense of pride and accomplishment helping these organizations and often engage in additional charitable actions in their personal lives." He concluded by saying, "In addition to the good feelings we gain, our sales have actually increased through our good works. This unexpected benefit came about because people were impressed with our work and wanted to use the same company who had produced such positive gains."

John Meyer,
CEO of Arise Virtual Solutions, courtesy of Arise Virtual Solutions

John Meyer, CEO of Arise Virtual Solutions, describes the company's approach to CSR, "Arise Virtual Solutions is in the business of changing the way the world works through its network of 25,000 home-based customer service professionals. The company aligns its social good efforts closely with its business goals, focusing its efforts on organizations whose focus is on the home and family." He explains the employee involvement, saying, "Our employees are extremely engaged and each year we look for a new initiative to support. This last year or so has been very focused on the Military Veterans community."

Meyer goes on to say, "Arise employees also participate in Habitat For Humanity builds throughout the United States several times a year, with plans to support international builds in the near future. Habitat for Humanity seeks to eliminate poverty housing and homelessness from the world. This partnership is a great fit for Arise, in particular, because of its corporate focus on 'home.'" He concluded with this observation, "During the actual Habitat For Humanity builds people get to spend the day with [employees] that perhaps (a) they have never met, (b) have never worked with, (c) have never had lengthy conversations with. We've also found that the teamwork required to build a house together is also carried over into the office."

Christy Consler, SVP of Human Resources and Corporate Sustainability, at Jamba Juice, says, "The Jamba-sponsored Team Up for a Healthy America program was launched in 2011 in an effort to raise awareness of the obesity epidemic in the United States and engage company partners in a broad awareness campaign aimed at encouraging and inspiring the nation's youth to make better dietary choices and providing ways for them to stay fit and keep active."

Consler adds, "From volunteering at local food banks, to running half marathons in support of charities and in support of employee's personal health goals, to participating in WNBA Fit Clinics at schools as part of Team Up, our employees are always active in driving our social responsibility programs."

Consler also notes, "Customers are highly engaged in our company's corporate social responsibility efforts because they recognize that Jamba is passionate about the impact they can have in their local communities. A few examples of how well our customers get involved would be their support of our current American Heart Association campaign in the Bay Area and our annual 'Pink Whirl' program to raise funds for the Susan G. Komen Foundation. In both cases, our customers overwhelmingly exceeded our donation goals."

Consler says, "As an example [of our success], our CEO was recently invited to speak with President Obama in a teleconference with 120 mayors from across the U.S. to describe our job hiring program aimed at creating summer employment opportunities for underserved youth through our nationwide National Hiring Day and our partnership with Job Corps of Treasure Island that offers culinary internships in our corporate headquarters."

With respect to the benefits of their social good efforts to the company, Consler concluded, "With our better-for-you offerings, our social responsibility programs and our ongoing support of the community, consumers continually recognize Jamba as one of the top health and wellness brands in the country, which is notable when you consider that we do not have stores in every state."

Perhaps the most encouraging sign amidst my research for this article was the tremendous number of companies I found that are making these efforts. It was impossible for me to include all the stories I found. As a result, I'll be writing a series of articles on this theme in the coming months. It does appear that the world is experiencing the beginning of what could become an era of more conscious capitalism.

If your company is doing good in the world, please leave a comment below explaining your initiative and the benefits your company receives from your good work.

Additional Resources

IF YOU FINISH this book and are looking for additional help and insights, let me first point you to my online course for Pluralsight. com. My two-hour course on *Adding Profit by Adding Purpose* there can help you and your team formulate a strategy and implement it.

Additionally, if you need help building consensus and enthusiasm for a program, I am available as a speaker to visit your organization to help get everyone moving in the same direction. Just email speaker@devinthorpe.com or call 801-210-2919. Visit devinthorpe.com to learn more about having me speak to your company.